This book is a
Gift

from

---

to

---

on the occasion of

---

date

---

i

DESTROYING MARITAL JINXES

-with **A PRAYER PLAN TO ARREST THE JINX MONSTER**

DR.D.K OLUKOYA

DECEMBER, 2015

Destroying Marital Jinxes

© 2015 DR. D. K. OLUKOYA

ISBN: 978-978-920-165-5

A publication of

Mountain of Fire and Miracles Ministries
International Headquarters, Lagos Nigeria.

TABLE *of* CONTENTS

vi

ONE

TRAPPED
AND
IGNORANT

TRAPPED AND IGNORANT

For you to be victorious in spiritual warfare, information is of great essence. Information is power, and the right type of information can bring freedom. That is why Jesus Christ says, **'And ye shall know the truth, and the truth shall make you free'.** *(John 8:32)*

Truth, which is essentially verified information, is key to solving most of life's many problems. Information is very important when you need to forge ahead in life. When you get to a juncture in life, where the road forks and leads in many directions, you need information.

There are problems in life that answer to *praise;* some answer to *prayers* and others answer to *knowledge;* still others respond to the *level of truth* or *information* that you know or possess. So when you have knowledge of divine truth, you are empowered with the requisite information to wage spiritual battles, and to forge ahead in the battles of life.

Until you know the truth and possess the information for tactical and strategic spiritual warfare, the enemy will make fun of your prayer efforts. At best, he will view you as a toothless bulldog which can only bark, but cannot bite. At worst, he will see you as a prince who does not have the key to the treasure room in his father's kingdom.

May you possess the knowledge of the truth to destroy the stronghold of the enemy in your life, in the name of Jesus.

The truth is a very powerful concept; it is the key that illuminates shrouded mysteries and provides a pathway in misted darkness. The truth, however, is useless if you do not know it. It is also of no value if you are unfortunate to move with friends or have a leader, who do not know the truth, especially spiritual truth.

Spiritual truth is the platform on which most of life's truth is built. As a matter of fact, and I say this with a burdened heart, there are lots of people who could be deemed monumental ignoramuses when it comes to spiritual matters; they profess spiritual inanities. The level of their ignorance, when it comes to spiritual matters is so deep that one can only shake his head in amazement. For example, some openly declare that there is nothing wrong about eating in the dream, adding that it may even fill in the gap for physical food. Others claim that there is nothing called generational curse. This is so sad!

Unfortunately, there are a lot of young people today that are being misled by these ignorant 'fathers in the Lord', 'pastors' 'mentors' and spiritual leaders'.

The truth however is that you need to arm yourself with spiritual knowledge in order to fulfill your destiny, which is being contested by many forces beyond your carnal or fleshly knowledge.

Another gem of truth we need to be aware of is that most of our ancestors did not serve the one and only true God. Rather, they served the devil with vigour and veracity. As a result of this, they plunged, not only themselves, but generations unborn, into everlasting bondage. This bondage is compounded by the shroud of ignorance that the devil is using to cover God's children nowadays.

This is made worse by the devil's emissaries, the self-styled spiritual leaders and pastors, who are helping him to propagate and perpetuate this bond of lies and ignorance. Because of this, children of God need to be very careful about what they watch, who they listen to or get counsel from.

This bond of ignorance can have a very strong grip over a life. If one chooses to buy into it, then one has voluntarily opted to stay in perpetual darkness. If a person does not take active step in destroying it, it will lead to spiritual cataract and deafness, which will cut one off from hearing and obeying the Will of heaven.

One particular area the devil has been exploiting and attacking the children of God in our world today is ignorance in the area of marriage. The prince of this world has almost bastardised the sanctum of the institution that God Himself established in the beautiful Garden of Eden (Gen.2:18; 21-24). The devil, through his hordes of agents and minions in different households of the world, has introduced satanic pronouncements to derail the marital destinies of many people. This is due, in large part, to the evil covenant entered into on their behalfs by their forefathers. These malevolent pronouncements then entered in the form of hexes and jinxes.

In the following pages, you will be learning about the mystery of jinxes, especially marital jinxes: what they are, the causes, their manifestations and the solution one can proffer to solving them.

As you read this manual, I pray that the Holy Spirit will open your eyes of understanding. If you have been trapped in the spiritual cage of ignorance, the spiritual truth of the Holy Spirit will make you free, and help you to avoid the   landmines of marital jinxes, in the name of Jesus.

CHAPTER

TWO

THE ANTAGONIST CALLED JINX

THE ANTAGONIST CALLED JINX

What is a jinx, and how does it manifest in the lives of people? How can you know or identify a jinxed marriage or relationship? What can be done to ameliorate or effectively cancel all the terrible effect of a jinxed marriage?

The problem of jinxes in marriages is not a matter to be taken lightly, as this satanic weapon of oppression has done untold harm to unsuspecting people all over the world, particularly to the body of Christ. Therefore, I pray that as you study this manual and say the accompanying prayers, your destiny will be positively impacted with the knowledge of the truth. As you learn from the feet of Christ the Master, He will break the yoke of marital jinx in your life, you shall obtain your marital breakthrough.

'*...but through knowledge shall the just be delivered*'. Prov.11:9b

'Buy the truth and sell it not; also wisdom, and instruction, and understanding' Prov.23:23

THE ANATOMY OF SPIRITUAL WARFARE

One of the first things a soldier needs to *know* in a warfare is, 'Who is the enemy?' There is absolutely no strategic sense in carrying a gun to the war-front when you, as a Christian soldier, do not know who your adversary is.

No matter how sophisticated a weapon is, and no matter how well-trained a soldier is, if he cannot identify the enemy, and on time too, he will be a danger to himself, and an easy prey to the invisible enemy, *'who walks about, like a roaring lion, seeking whom he may devour"(I Peter 5:8)*.

Many people are praying, but it is unfortunate that they are not getting commensurate results. This is because they do not pray divinely-directed and targeted prayers. They have not carried out what can be called a *spiritual diagnosis* of their lives to know what exactly is afflicting them. So they pray in ignorance or pray the wrong kind of prayers. This makes them to end up with sore knees and frustrated lives.

In military warfare, there is something called 'sharp-shooting'. This is the act of attaining a high degree of proficiency in the use of shooting and hitting a target, whether moving or stationary, and becoming a good marksman. In spiritual warfare, we also need to learn to do what we may call *spiritual sharp-shooting*. That is the only way we can wage a successful war against the robbers of marital successes.

But if you are not well-informed and have truth as your guide, your warring with prayers may not be totally effective. Hence, your need to pray informed and directed prayers. Information *transforms* a man, while the lack of information *deforms* and destroys him.

When you lack spiritual information, you are just an accident waiting to happen. You could be born again for years, but if you are not privileged to know certain spiritual truths, you will remain in spiritual oblivion.

Spiritual treasures are not found on the surface. Like physical treasures, they are found only in the deep; spiritual treasures are designed only for those who are ready to dig deep, for those who have the grit and determination to succeed, and who will not settle for anything less than God's best.

Most times, you need access to certain details before you can lay claim to the treasures. You need spiritual information in your quest for fulfillment in life, especially in marital fulfillment.

For wisdom is a defence, and money is a defence, but the excellency of knowledge is that wisdom giveth life to them that have it. (Eccl. 7:12)

A man once went for prayers over a problem that proved stubborn. As the man of God started praying with him, he heard God speak. God said the root of the man's problem is in the family praise-name given to him and he should go and ask his parents more about it. He went home and made enquiries from his parents who affirmed this. In his case, the devil has turned the family praise-name, what the Yoruba call *oriki*, into a jinx, or an albatross, to tie his marital destiny down. But the noteworthy thing is that, he never knew about it until God disclosed it. After this disclosure, the Lord set him free from his afflictions.

The Bible says in the book of Deuteronomy:"***The secret things belong unto the Lord our God, but those things which are revealed belong unto us and to our children for ever...***"(Deut.29:29a)

This was like the case of Jonah. He was running away from God and as a result, the Lord stirred up the sea against the ship he boarded. The lives of everyone on board were at stake, until they discovered that Jonah was the cause of their woes. He was a jinx to their lives. Not until they threw him out of the ship did the raging sea calm down (Jonah 1:4-16). Likewise, if you do not discover the 'Jonah' in the boat of your marital destiny, progress in life will be very difficult, or even impossible.

WHAT IS A JINX?

1. A jinx is a person, a thing or a set of circumstances that brings bad-luck or misfortune.
2. It is an evil spell or influence over somebody.
3. It is a power that brings misfortune.
4. It is a condition of bad-luck.
5. A jinx is anything that invites misfortune into a life or the lives of others.

WHAT DOES IT MEAN TO BE JINXED?

➢ To place a curse on
➢ To bewitch
➢ To enchant
➢ To possess

➤ To bring misfortune on something

I used to have a colleague while I was working as a scientist. Anytime something good was coming his way, some food items will be sent to him from his village. Once he eats the food, that will be the end of the impending breakthrough. For no reason at all, the door of success would just close against him, and he would go back to square one.

Whether it is an interview, a meeting, an appointment or other engagement that had been earmarked to bring him promotion and bless his life, once the food from his home-villageare brought in, and he devoured these foods, there will be no recorded success. This is an example of a jinxed life. And the food has been made a jinx for him.

THE JINX OF ACHAN

Some materials or object that people erroneously bring into their lives can also introduce a jinx and bring ill-luck to them and others. A classic biblical case is that of the covetous Achan, whose greed led to the jinx on an entire nation.

But the children of Israel committed a trespass in the accursed thing: for Achan, the son of Carmi, the son of Zabdi, the son of Zerah, of the tribe of Judah, took of the accursed thing: and the anger of the LORD was kindled against the children of Israel. (Joshua 7:1)

Achan took something he should not. This was against the commandment of God, and he became a jinx to the children of Israel. Until they destroyed Achan and his house, the children of Israel could not make any progress. This means something you brought into your house can constitute a jinx.

And Achan answered Joshua, and said, Indeed I have sinned against the Lord God of Israel and thus and thus have I done: When I saw among the spoils a goodly Babylonish garment, and two hundred shekels of silver, and a wedge of gold of fifty shekels weight, then I coveted them and took them; and, behold, they are hid in the earth in the midst of my tent, and the silver under it.(Joshua 7:20-21)

NEGATIVE HUMAN MAGNET

It is not only *material things* that can become a jinx. Human beings, too, like the case of Achan above, can be jinxed, or can be used as a jinx for others. Some people have a run of ill-luck such that when they enter into a relationship, things may look promising at the initial stages, but suddenly the people they are in relationship with begin to experience multiple attacks which they find strange and incomprehensible. There could be a jinx of ill-luck operating in the life of such a person. This person may have been turned into a negative human magnet by the forces of darkness. A jinx could have been planted in the life of such a person to make him or her to be attracting the wrong suitors or partners.

SOME BIBLICAL EXAMPLES OF JINXES

➢ **Delilah was a jinx to Samson.** Samson was a covenant child, and a Nazirite of God. But he became careless with his destiny and allowed a jinx, Delilah, to walk into his life. Delilah, a sultry beauty, had a very clear agenda and she literally told Samson; '*show me the secret of your power so that I candestroy you*'. (Judges **16**:6). This was a clear warning to Samson to flee, but because Delilah was a jinxsent by the forces of darkness, and because of his spiritual blindness, he did not listen. Neither did he respond to the promptings of the Spirit of God which was upon his life. The result? He ended up dying with his enemies, with his eyesgouged out.

(Judges **16**:1-22)

➢ **Lot was a jinx to Abraham.** God commanded Abraham to get out of his father's house, and from his idolatrous family and nation. But in his ignorance, he took his worldly nephew Lot, with him. Lot became an albatross to Abraham in his way of making tangible progress. As long as Abraham allowed Lot to be attached to him, he didn't make any meaningful progress. First, he had to put up with Lot's quarrelsome herdsmen. Later, he had to rescue Lot from a raiding party. All these considerably slowed Abraham's own progress(Gen.**13**:7-13; **14**:14-16)

➤ **Judas was a jinx to the Lord Jesus Christ:** Despite the fact that Judas was with Jesus for a period of three years, (some Bible scholars even aver that he is a distant relative of Christ: they both come from the tribe of Judah), that did not stop the devil from using him as a jinx (a traitor) against Christ.(John **18**:2-5)

➤ **Herod constituted a great jinx to the early church, when he killed Apostle James and persecuted the rest.** In order to appease the Jews and curry their favour, both for political gains and pecuniary purposes, Herod raised his hand against the young church in Jerusalem and killed James and sent the others into hiding.(Acts **12**:1-12)

➤ **Saul was a jinx to the early Christians:** Saul of Tarsus was a mighty thorn in the flesh of the Christians in Jerusalem and he collaborated in the killing of Stephen, until Jesus Christ arrested him on the road to Damascus, and commissioned him an apostle to the Gentiles. (Acts **9**:1-16; **26**:14-18)

Perhaps, the greatest jinx that could be placed upon a person is the one from his own family, as happened in the case of Manasseh.

Joseph brought his two children, Manasseh and Ephraim, to his father Jacob for blessings. Normally, in the Jewish tradition, the grandfather is expected to lay his right hand on the elder, and his left hand on the younger. Because of this, Joseph placed the firstborn on the right hand position of his father and the younger child on the left hand side. However, to

the amazement of Joseph, his aged father who could not see properly crossed his hands. He placed the right hand on the younger child instead, and the left hand on the firstborn. Joseph protested thinking his father made a mistake, but the old man said 'not so' and insisted that Joseph should let it be.
(Genesis 48:8-22)

This might be thought of as the power of jinxes saying 'no' to the right thing in the life of Manasseh, the elder child of Joseph. Years later, because the blessings of the first-born had passed on to Ephraim the younger, he prospered and waxed much stronger, ten times more, than Manasseh. (Deut.33:17b)

'His glory is like the firstling of his bullock.....and they are the TEN THOUSANDS of Ephraim and they are the THOUSANDS of Manasseh'

In essence, a jinx is the negative power saying 'no' to one's breakthroughs and prosperity. It is the power that is resisting the advancement of a person. It is the power of satanic immigration officers at the border of an individual's Promised Land, saying someone cannot gain access. It is the power contending for one's victory. It is the power that has been delegated to stagnate and frustrate a soul. It is the power that is sad to see a person make progress and for no particular reason or offense. It is the power that is bent on keeping someone in a situation that makes him or her perpetually unhappy. A Jinx is the evil angel assigned to frustrate a person. It is the power of the night that manipulates breakthroughs through negative dreams.

A jinx is the power circulating one's name for evil, stealing a person's good things, and swallowing his or her opportunities. It is the power that nullifies the program of God for a life; it is the power that is assigned to chase away someone's divine helpers and make him to invite irritation and anger instead of joy. It is the power that siphons a person's virtues and programmes a negative aura around the person so that those that should come around to add value to his or her life are distracted and kept very far away from him. Jinxes are the powers that rage when you are close to your breakthrough and suddenly you begin to see an otherwise peaceful relationship slip away from your hands without a genuine reason. They are the powers that will remove your name from the profitable list and place it on the losers' chart. They are the powers that will enforce evil utterance upon a life. All these are the evil works of a jinx. A jinx puts a stamp of ill-luck upon a life; to delay, and to ultimately deny the life of the wonderful things that the Lord has made for his or her benefits. A man, in ignorance, may be blaming Providence and may even be prompted by unfriendly friends to *'curse God and die'*(Job 2:9b).But if he can stay faithful to the word of God, which says, in Jeremiah 30:8:

'For it shall come to pass in that day, saith the LORD of hosts, that I will break his yoke from off thy neck, and I will burst thy bounds.........,

The Lord will break all the yokes of satanic jinx and set him free from the clutches of the enemy.

A jinx is a very terrible thing because it keeps the jinxed individual stagnant. It keeps him redundant and makes him to ramble in the market-square of life. One important thing you must know is that anything can be used as a jinx. Fortunately, **there are three proven and time-tested antidotes that CAN be effectively used to destroy any jinx.**

These are:

(1)   the *name* of the Lord Jesus Christ,

(2)   the Blood of Jesus, and

(3)   the word of God.

'Wherefore God also hath highly exalted him, and given him A NAME which is above every name; that at THE NAME OF JESUS every knee should bow, of things in heaven, and things in earth, and things under the earth' (Phil.2:9-10,Emphasis added)

'And they overcame him by THE BLOOD OF THE LAMB, and by THE WORD of their testimony; and they loved not their lives unto the death' (Rev.12: 11, Emphasis added)

'For the WORD OF GOD is quick, and powerful, and sharper than any two-edged sword, piercing even to the dividing asunder of soul and spirit...'(Heb.4:12, Emphasis added)

There are several jinxes that the enemy is using to afflict the world today, including even the children of God in the Church.

These will be expounded in the subsequent pages.

THREE

MAJOR MARITAL JINXES

MAJOR MARITAL JINXES

1.   *The invisible jinx.*

Here you are: an attractive and beautiful lady, sociable, appealing, sophisticated and qualified. You have all it takes to captivate, win and keep a man's heart but nobody seems to notice you, let alone ask your hand in marriage. The satanic powers have simply made you 'invisible' and people that should give you rapt attention just pass by without deigning to look at you.

This was the case of a sister who was a banker. She graduated with a very good grade, and started working in one of the financial discount houses on Lagos Island. She had everything a man could desire in a life partner, but curiously and mysteriously, no man seemed to be asking even her name. Over the years she got several promotions at work and moved up the career ladder, yet her marital destiny seemed to be on hold.

It was at this point that she cried out to the Lord in prayer. A friend of hers who is a member of Mountain of Fire and Miracles Ministries brought her for deliverance, and while the prayer was going on, the Lord revealed to the man of God that a veil had been cast upon her spiritually by her father's sister, her aunt, who had vowed that she would never marry in life. This wicked woman, who was into witchcraft, placed a marital jinx on her to the effect that men who were supposed to woo her and ask for her hand in marriage would be looking at her, but they would not 'see' her.

After the mandatory three-daydry fasting with targeted prayers, the Lord further revealed that the perpetrator of this evil act had committed the satanic act when this sister was at the University. The Lord delivered her by destroying the spiritual veil placed upon her to prevent potential suitors from 'seeing' her. This completely destroyed the power of the jinx which was placed upon her and brought the ordeal of the sister to an end.

Three months after this, she met a sophisticated young man, who had come to Nigeria after nine years of study in Australia. The young man proposed to her and a year later, they were married, to the glory of God.

Every evil veil, placed upon me, to deny me of my spiritual blessing, your time is up, die, in the name of Jesus!!

2.   *The touch-and-go jinx.*

This is a kind of jinx in which all the men that meets with the lady just want to sleep with her, dust their trousers and depart, like a stray dog. Conversely too, if the jinx is on a man, then all the ladies that come around him may just want a taste of him s e x u a l l y, milk him a little bit if he has money and just go away when they have had enough of him. In other words, they are not interested in marriage; they just want a bit of fun and of his gravy and they are gone! In some cases, the lady who wants to prove smart may get herself impregnated by such a man who will of course deny the responsibility outright.

The jinx can also take the form of 'I like-you-but-I-don't-love-you'. In other words, they like the body, money and the material possession the victim has, but not the thing most needed, that is, the love and commitment that will lead to a marital commitment. They live off the victim for a while and then disappear. This is a terrible jinx from the darkest pit of hell, and it has left many young men and young women frustrated and disenchanted with relationships generally.

You will not be a prey for the devil, to be used and dumped, like a filthy rag, in the name of Jesus.

3. *Domineering parents jinx.*

This is the jinx that comes into play when all the marital choices you make are opposed and rubbished by one or both parents. Anybody you bring home as a would-be partner is rejected, condemned or rebuffed by the father, the mother or both.

Sometimes, the enemy uses the parents as a jinx against the child. Some children are actually under the bondage of parental soul-tie which they mistake for 'parental love'. This is because they have not been completely weaned from the domineering grip of one or both parents, who run their lives as children by making decisions for them, including that of a marriage partner. This is not a healthy development.

The fact is that some men and women are still tied to their parents' apron strings, and they cannot make any impactful nor meaningful decision without involving such parents.

Most times, the parents have hidden motives or agendas concerning the type of daughter-in-law or son-in-law they want in their family. Take for instance, a jealous or a possessive mother whose son brings home a beautiful and educated young lady, to be introduced to her as a future wife. The mother may feel threatened by the endowments and accomplishments of the young lady and sees her only as someone who is coming to snatch or steal her son from her. Once she begins to feel this threat, she will do everything in her power to ensure that the marital union does not take place. She constitutes herself into an opposition party in the family.

There was a case of a mother who opposed all the young women her son brought home for marriage. It became so bad that the remaining maidens in the village started avoiding the young man, asking him to go and marry his mother.

In some African families, it has been discovered that some parents actually use witchcraft powers to influence the decisions of their children's choices in marriage. This becomes a great jinx on the otherwise incompatible partners who come under the influence of evil powers. These powers will later plant a negative seed in the lives of the couple in order to tear the marriage apart. It is not only abnormal but weird when parents impose their will on their children or wards on marital issues. Marital progress will be very difficult for such people.

Another terrible version of this jinx, is the case of children who do not even think of getting married at all, but prefer to live in the overprotective shadows of their parents. The mother can even be calling the son, 'my husband'. In this way some parents have ended up marrying their children spiritually, thus making it impossible for the children to marry physically. This is a terrible jinx in the life of the child-victim.

4. *The dream-marriage jinx.*

This is the kind of jinx which manifests itself when you only see yourself getting married in the dream while there is nothing close to that in the physical. The purpose of this jinx is to keep the victim engaged in the spirit realm and to make him unavailable to his or her divinely-ordained partner in the physical realm. This is a very sad and frustrating issue especially when the victim has prayed and fasted, but is still unaware that there is an evil covenant that must be broken to free him from such demonic dream marriage. The problem is compounded when, as often is the case, it involves a spirit wife/spirit husband.

5. *The spirit-spouse jinx.*

Some spirit beings are at the root of many a jinx of marital delays. The spirit wife, or a *succubus*, which is a female demon and the spirit husband, or *incubus*, a male demon, attach themselves to human spouses in what is generally regarded as legal marriage in the spiritual realm.

These spirit beings enter into the lives of the human male or female through the sin of fornication, or some other immoral lifestyle, or through an ancestral shrine to which the victim has been dedicated, as a child.

Unfortunately, many people have become silent sufferers as a result of the activities of these beings, popularly known as spirit wives and spirit husbands. This is becoming more and more prevalent in this end-time when the devil is unleashing terror from all cylinders.

Some people unwittingly put themselves into the yoke and the jinx of the spirit spouses by seeking solutions where there is none. Some visit herbalists, false prophets and satanic mar abouts. Others indulge in unholy river baths, visit shrines, engage in ritualistic and ancestral festivals; participate in eating from the devil's tables or join evil associations.

Some men enter into covenant relationship with the devil, in their bid to get rich quick. In the case of some women, they go to forbidden places when they are looking for the fruit of the womb. These mark such life for a jinx.

The devil, who is a wily negotiator, and the brain behind all such ungodly transactions, enters into a covenant relationship with them, to their detriment. Part of this evil covenant is that they are married off to the demon-being which is actually the spirit behind such shrine or coven they visited. This places a marital jinx on these hapless victims and their unborn offsprings.

It must be admitted though, that most of these covenants are entered into in ignorance. But then, in the spirit realm, ignorance is not an excuse. That is why children of God need to harm themselves with the truth of God's word.

In the case of a man, the succubus or spirit wife, who is extremely jealous and fatally possessive, will defend her human husband from all physical(and spiritual)intruders,even to the point of death. She will, for instance, afflict the male intruder with stagnancy, joblessness, poverty and even sicknesses. All these are done to keep the man useless and redundant, so that he could not fend for himself, talk less of getting married and settling down. Men in such conditions have been known to say they will never marry. Such negative confessions are used by the devil to compound their woes, and to place an embargo on their marital destinies.

For a married couple, the spirit wife will torment the marriage with many problems that defy solutions. The spirit wife could cause the couple, for instance, to hate each other so much that it could cause the couple to be barren, which could eventually lead to separation or divorce.

This is a serious source of marital jinx, and it is most common in the riverine areas.

Any ancestral evil spirit-wife/husband, assigned to bring me down, you are a liar, die, in the name of Jesus!!

6.   *The Evil family-pattern jinx.*

This jinx typifies a family situation in which all the members are having similar experiences in one area of their lives –marriage. You could call it a jinx of collective captivity.

The family members will move in a vicious cycle without achieving the much-needed marital breakthrough. If you find yourself in such a predicament, and you realize that your parents went through the same ordeal, you should know at once that you have a terrible jinx to break. And the jinx could manifest in different guises:

SOME COMMON FAMILY JINXES
Father-daughter jinx. In some cases, some daughters are so attached to their fathers that the

DESTROYING MARITAL JINXES

spirit of the father would not want to release them in marriage. This is a jinx arising from the soul of the father which is tied to that of her daughter. Most times, those affected are ignorant of this jinx. Everybody says the lady is daddy's pet, but in truth, it goes beyond that. It's a jinx that needs to be broken.

The mother-son jinx. In this case, the son is so attached to his mother to the extent that he surrenders to her decisions that even he, as a man, is supposed to make. Whatever the mother decides is what he does. This is why if she opposes the girl he brings home as a future partner, he doesn't kick, he simply folds up and sends the girl away. In some cases, such sons may actually be under demonic influence so much that the devil will manipulate them into sleeping with the mother. This is a serious incestuous relationship that is punishable under divine law for up to ten generations. It is a satanic jinx from the pit of hell.

The sibling jinx. Another variation of the family jinx is the sibling jinx. Here, a family member, the brother or sister introduces a future partner to his or her siblings, but before long, one of the siblings snatches the new introduction into the family. Of course, this is evil, absolutely satanic. It will certainly breed resentment and bitterness that will, at the end of the day, scatter the marriage. This is a great jinx, which if discovered early, should be destroyed on the altar of prayer.

This is especially rampant in polygamous families where there is a spirit of strife, bitterness, jealousy and a pull-him-down syndrome. This root of competition and envy gives the devil a leeway to plant a jinx in the family which puts all the unwary members in bondage.

"And a man's foes shall be they of his own household". Matthew 10:36

7. *The negative-magnet jinx.*

This kind of jinx attracts wrong people to the person. Thus women under the evil influence of this particular jinx get attracted to married men, polygamous men, and undesirable elements in the society such as touts, pimps, drop-outs, party-crawlers etc.

And he went and joined himself to a citizen of that country; and he sent him into his fields to feed the swine. Luke 15:15

In this unfortunate situation, the enemy has placed a negative spiritual magnet on such a victim, and anywhere she turns to, she will be attracting or pulling to herself the most undesirable partners.

This is a serious spiritual matter and until such soul cries out to the Lord, this evil trend will continue to plague her.

Every evil mirror, that the enemy is using to introduce ill-luck into my life, break, in the name of Jesus.

This particular jinx also manifests as the tragedy jinx. With the tragedy jinx, there are always occurrences that bring tragic consequences with a potential to scatter a marriage or relationship.

There was a case of a sister who lived in South Africa. Anytime she did the formal introduction of her fiancé to members of her family, the result is always tragic: the fiancé died either in an accident or of a strange sickness a little while later. This happened four times until a friend directed her to the headquarters of the Mountain of Fire and Miracles Ministries in Lagos to see the General Overseer. It was here at the MFM that the Lord finally met her at the point of her marital needs. The Lord destroyed the barrier of death-and-hell spirit jinx that the enemy of her father's house had placed on her.

8. *The armed-robbery jinx.*

Here, you find someone you love and you are in a serious relationship. Then suddenly, from nowhere, a man appears in the scene, says he is seriously in love with the same woman, then snatches her and before your very eyes, they are gone! At first, you are left speechless, then you explode in a rage, when it suddenly occurs to you that this is not the first time such will be happening in the family.

The jinx could also take another form: You discover that armed robbers are attacking your properties, especially your wedding materials. They may not be disappearing in one fell swoop but bit by bit, and you can't understand how. Then, know that the devil has set a trap for your marital destiny. You need to raise your hands to the Lord in prayer.

Then there is the *envy jinx*. Here, anything you have, and whatever you become attracts envy of the people around you. This brings inexplicable hatred towards you, without reason and without any explanation whatsoever. When this happens, know that you are operating under an iron-clad jinx that needs to be shattered with the force of warfare prayers.

9. *The Delay jinx.*

'Hope deferred maketh the heart sick' Proverbs 13:12

Delay causes infirmity of the heart: it makes the heart sick. The devil uses delay to discourage, denyand often to destroy the marital joy of many people. How does he do this? The devil is an expert psychologist, and quite knowledgeable in the ways and manners of men. He knows perfectly well that most men hate waiting, so he afflicts their destinies with the arrows of delay, especially in the area of marriage, so that in their impatience, they make wrong choices.

Hence, receiving a promise of God for a marital breakthrough should never make you go to sleep. This is because the devil is not going to leave you alone. Since he knows who your future or marriage partner is, he will do everything either to keep the two of you from meeting each other, or he may fill her heart with doubts or anything that will make the final decision to linger on and on, all in a bid to delay the divine arrangement coming to fruition.

10. *The Poverty jinx.*

Immediately the man who is jinxed with poverty enters into a relationship, the first thing that will probably happen to him is to lose his job, that is, his means of livelihood. In some extreme cases, armed robbers could pay him a visit or a fire disaster that claims his properties may occur. All this is to unsettle the man and financially throw him out of balance. But in some cases, the man may not be the direct attack of the jinx. Sometimes, it could be the woman he wants to marry or has married. She could be thrown into some financial mess which the man, if he loves her, would want to help resolve. This way, even if the man is free from the jinx, he will nonetheless suffer loss, both financially and emotionally. This is certainly not the best way to start a home. But you must not sit and relax and moan. The moment you realize such manifestation in your relationship, you must fight like a wounded lion until you snatch victory from the jaws of the enemy.

11. *The free-for-all jinx.*

This means a man attracts too many women into his life (or in case of a woman, too many men into her life). Such women simply live only for the moment. They siphon from the poor man as much as they can and they are gone. Other than the poor consolation that he takes them to bed, he does not get anything else in return because he does not get any commitment by way of a workable relationship with any of them. Like a terrible nightmare, the women flow in from everywhere, enter and exit his life at will. At the end, he is sapped dry and dumped. He is not even given any opportunity to develop a really serious relationship that could lead to marriage. So he is stuck, living the life of a frustrated ageing bachelor.

12. *The Covenant jinx.*

When you find yourself entering into series of covenants with different people over marital issues, and nothing concrete is coming out of it each time, know for sure that you are under the covenant jinx. Most times, the covenant you enter into with one person does not sustain the relationship, and before you know it, you are with another person and talking about another covenant. This is a jinx.

The book of Psalms 74:20 says:

'*...have respect unto the covenant; for the dark places of this earth are full of the habitations of cruelty*'

13. *The polygamy jinx.*

Individuals from polygamous families are already at a disadvantage in marital choices from birth because of inborn marital jinx. People who come from this type of background often find it difficult to keep a healthy and sound relationship. Women from such background experience multiple proposals that lead nowhere, while for the men, the marital journey is often bumpy and complicated. There is always a negative exodus from one partner to the other.

The truth is that if you are from a polygamous family or background, know for certain that you have a serious marital jinx to cancel before you can enter into your marital breakthrough.

Another dimension to this polygamy jinx is as a result of the activity of witchcraft which is rampant within the structure. Most of the witchcraft battles that are raging in many families today are fertilized on the soil of polygamy. That is why the Bible says that a man who wants to serve on the altar of the Lord must be the husband of one wife.

" If a man desire the office of a bishop, he desireth a good work.(He) must be blameless, THE HUSBAND OF ONE WIFE... "
(1 Tim.3:1-2, Emphasis added)

You must do everything within your power to break this jinx for the wind of marital freedom to blow into your destiny.

14. *The break-up jinx.*

This is when all your relationships just mysteriously end in break-ups. A woman recently brought her daughter to see me. This young lady has had thirteen broken engagements. She was distraught when she got to my office for counseling.

The problem she was having was that she had a serious jinx in her life that was responsible for all the disasters she was suffering in her relationships with men. After seeking the face of the Lord, His word came and it brought a solution to her life and accelerated her marital destiny. Now she is enjoying marital bliss.

Every satanic power, attempting to deny you victory in the area of marital breakthrough, I command them to die, in the name of Jesus!

Interest-famine jinx is another form of the break-up jinx. Here the relationship starts with much excitement and pomp, then suddenly all the excitement fizzles out and the couple discovers that they don't have interest in the relationship anymore, and this for no tangible reason! It's simply that they no longer have the interest of being together again. This is caused by the seed of bitterness, doubts, and unexplainable hatred sown into the relationship by the enemy. It is not unreasonable in such a relationship to discover that each partner has lived through broken relationships in the past. In such a situation, the present relationship cannot be expected to be different. It is a terrible jinx which each partner must deal with if they want to have a marital fulfillment.

This jinx is responsible for many of the divorces that are being experienced in the world today. If not handled properly at the prenuptial stage, they form a dark ladder for the enemy to climb into the union to plant tares and sorrow.

The enemy will not sow tares, sorrow and tragedy in your marriage, in the name of Jesus.

15. *The liar jinx.*

Some people live in a marital structure built on and sustained by lies. Some engage in marriage rackets, fake marriages, and false identity and so on, for various selfish reasons.

This type of behaviour places a jinx on the perpetrators of these evil acts as they are defiling the honourable institution that God has put in place to bless and replenish the earth. This has a serious repercussion on these ones and their coming generation.

I pray that the curse of God will not be upon you and yours, in the name of Jesus.

16. *The closed-door jinx.* God has a time-table of marital success for all his children. It is normal that at a right age, every man or woman makes connections that will lead to marriage. At this stage, the young man would search out the woman he will want to introduce to some close members of his family as his choice in marriage.

In the case of a woman, it is also expected that she would introduce a man to her parents as her choice for marriage. But when nothing of the sort is happening over a reasonable period of time in the life of the man or woman, then there is a cause for worry. Most likely it is a case of a closed-door jinx, which simply means that there is a hidden jinx in the life of the man or woman which needs to be broken. In such a situation, the first step to take would be to seek the counsel of a man of God, preferably a deliverance minister, who will through prayer of enquiries break the jinx. Without this, it will be very difficult to experience open heavens and open doors for a fruitful marriage.

17. *The vampire jinx*.

A vampire is a living corpse that rises from its grave to feed upon the blood or the life-sap of its victim. Men and women who prey on their partners are vampires. For example, a woman who sucks her lover dry and leaves him in a state of penury, wretchedness, financial and social degradation is a vampire. A nagging wife is also a vampire because the overall effect of nagging is to wear and sap the strength of the other. In the same way, a wife-battering husband could also be labeled a vampire.

Different shades of the vampires exist in our contemporary world. For example, we have child molesters. There are also the cheats who preys on the innocence of their wives. The vampire jinx has the same end-result: this is to degrade, weaken and render ineffective the personality of the other. In all the above cases, this type of jinx is at work to drain the potent life of the victims.

Every satanic agenda to milk the juice of your marital destiny will meet with failure, in the name of Jesus.

From this moment onward, I plug your life into the socket of divine favour that will accelerate your marital breakthrough, in the name of Jesus.

FOUR

A QUEST FOR FREEDOM

A QUEST FOR FREEDOM

The first thing you must do in order to obtain freedom from all forms of marital jinxes is to surrender your life to Jesus. This is very important and non-negotiable. It is only after taking this vital and destiny-impacting decision that you are recognized as a covenant child and a joint-heir of the kingdom of God.

The next thing you need do is to look for a Spirit-filled and Bible-believing church of God where you can receive spiritual nourishment and grow as a disciple of the Lord Jesus Christ. While doing this, the Holy Spirit will nudge you towards the areas of life where you need prayers and deliverance. The Holy Spirit will also raise help for you in the relevant areas in order to break stubborn and long-standing generational jinxes, which will set you free from marital bondages and satanic delays.

Finally, you will need to barricade your life with the Blood of Jesus (Rev.12:11) and the fire of the Holy Ghost (Acts 2:3) so that the fiery darts of the enemy's jinxes will no more have a landing space in your life.

I pray as you take this step of faith, that marital breakthroughs and open doors will be your lot, in the name of Jesus.

Marital jinx and delays will never be your portion again, in the name of Jesus.

CHAPTER

ONE

A PRAYER PLAN TO CRUSH MARITAL JINXES

A PRAYER PLAN TO CRUSH MARITAL JINXES

1. Every jinx, affecting my marital breakthrough, break, in the name of Jesus.

2. My long-awaited marital success, appear, in the name of Jesus.

3. Powers, contesting for my marital destiny, your time is up: die, in the name of Jesus.

4. (Point your right hand into the heavens and decree;) Every satanic immigration officer in the second heaven lies, at the border-post of my marital breakthrough, fall down and die, in the name of Jesus.

5. My wedding gown, in the custody of Queen of the Coast, be released, by the precious Blood of the Lamb.

6. You the strongman/strongwoman of my father's house, holding the key to my marital joy, receive the arrows from the throne-room of God and die, in the name of Jesus.

7. Angels of the Living God, go into the covens of darkness, and retrieve my marital glory, in the name of Jesus.

8. Heavens over my marital joy, be opened, and remain permanently open, in the name of Jesus.

9. Rain of joy; begin to fall on my destiny, in the name of Jesus.

10. Shower of marital blessing, my life is available, fall on me, in the name of Jesus.

11. All my anticipated marital bliss, manifest, in the name of Jesus.

12. Powers, sitting on my marital destiny, be unseated by the fire of God, in the name of Jesus.

13. East Wind of God, blow and shatter into pieces, the evil plans of the enemy concerning my marital life, in the name of Jesus.

14. Triangular powers in the heaven lies, (the sun, the moon and the stars), refuse to cooperate

with my enemies, in the name of Jesus.

15. O God of Elijah, arise in your wrath, and consume all the accuser of my marital success, in the name of Jesus.

16. My marital glory, appear by fire from the camp of the enemy, in the name of Jesus.

17. Everything that the Lord created, cooperate with the glory of my marriage, in the name of Jesus.

18. Cloud of affliction over my marriage, clear away, in the name of Jesus.

19. Any rage of spirit wife/spirit husband over my marital joy, be silenced, in the name of Jesus.

20. Every evil hand, planning to attack my marriage, wither by fire, in the name of Jesus.

21. O God my father, demonstrate your eternal love for my marriage, in the name of Jesus.

www.ingramcontent.com/pod-product-compliance
Lightning Source LLC
Chambersburg PA
CBHW060147050426
42448CB00010B/2338